Perseverance!

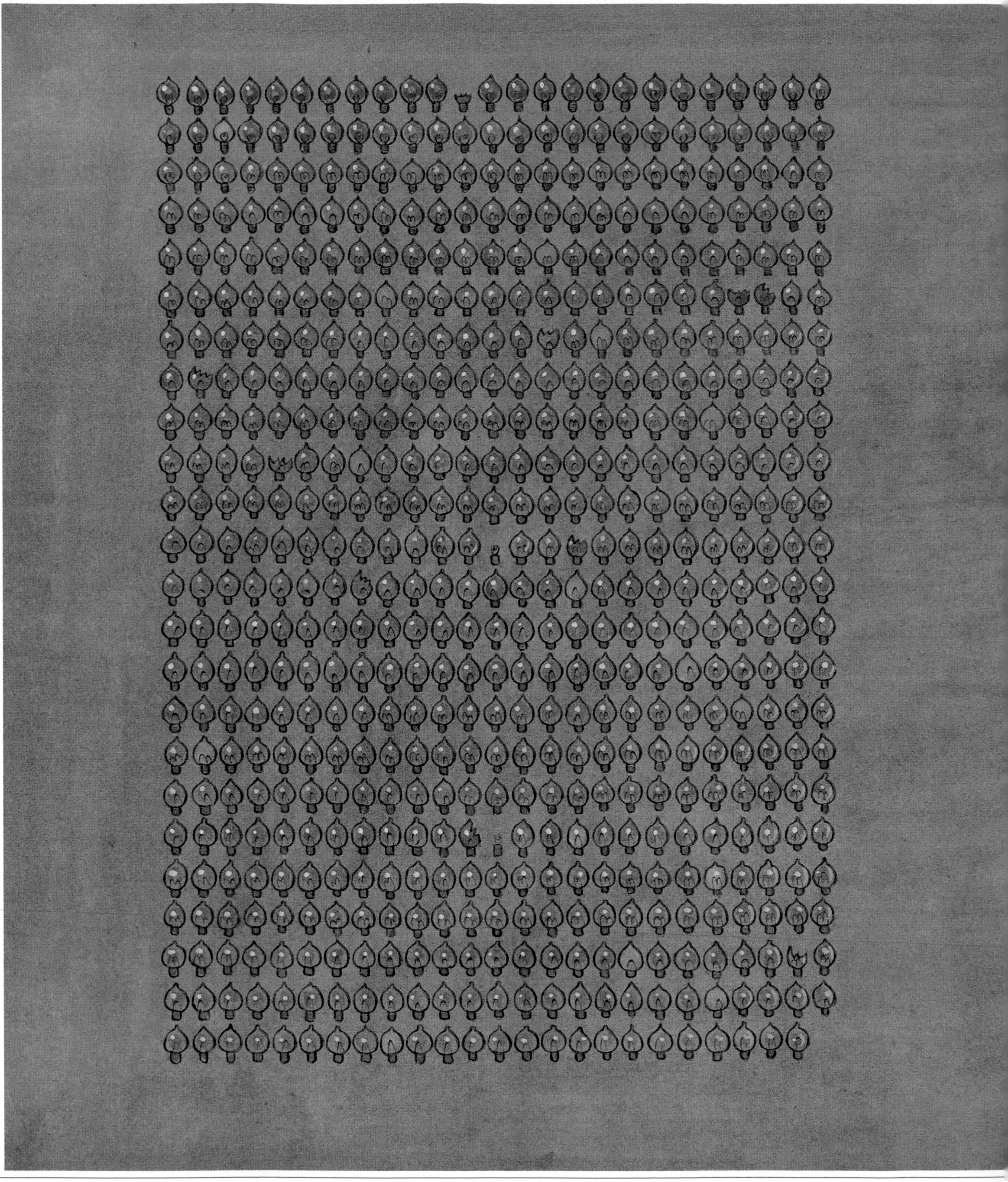

Perseverance!

The Story of Thomas Alva Edison

by

Peter Murray

Illustrated by

Robin Lawrie

The Child's World®

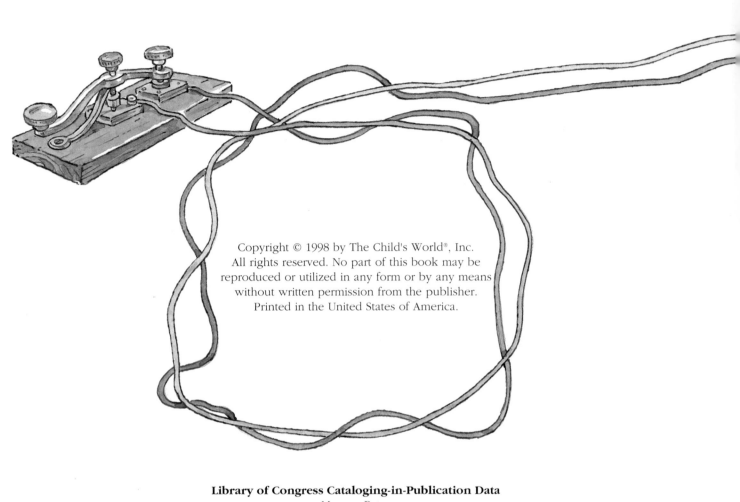

Library of Congress Cataloging-in-Publication Data
Murray, Peter
Perseverance: the story of Thomas Alva Edison / Peter Murray.
p. cm.
Summary: Traces the life of the man who invented the phonograph, light
bulb, and the motion picture camera, with an emphasis on the value of
perseverance in his achievements

ISBN 1-56766-228-5

1. Edison, Thomas A. (Thomas Alva), 1847-1931--Juvenile literature.
2. Inventors--United States-- Biography--Juvenile literature. 3.
Perseverance (Ethics)--Juvenile literature.
[1. Edison, Thomas A (Thomas Alva), 1847-1931. 2. Inventors.] I. Title.
TK 140.E3M85 1996
621.3'092
[B]--DC20
95-44358
CIP
AC r96

Contents

Edison's First Experiment

Mrs. Edison could not find her four-year-old son anywhere.

"I wonder where he is," she said.

She called his name, but no one answered.

She looked in his room, but he wasn't there.

She looked in the shed, but he wasn't there either.

She looked in the cellar. She looked under the porch. She could not find him anywhere. But she knew if she kept looking, she would find him.

She looked in the barn. The mother goose saw her and honked and flapped its wings. The goose was angry. Someone had taken over her nest!

"Thomas Alva Edison," Mrs. Edison said. "Why are you sitting in the goose's nest?"

"I saw the goose sitting on her eggs," said the boy. "I thought if I did the same thing, I could hatch baby geese, too."

Mrs. Edison said, "You never stop trying things, do you?"

That night Mrs. Edison told Mr. Edison what their son had done. She said, "You know, if I hadn't made him get off that nest, I believe he would have sat there until those eggs hatched!"

Mr. Edison laughed. "When that boy gets his mind set on something, he just won't quit."

What Is *Perseverance?*

The dictionary defines *perseverance* as "steady persistence in following a course of action, a belief, or a purpose. Steadfastness."

But what does that *mean?* It means you don't give up. When you run into a problem, you just keep on trying. And you don't quit, even when you're behind.

The Young Scientist

Thomas Alva Edison was born on February 11, 1847, in Milan, Ohio. We now think of him as Thomas Edison, but when he was a boy everybody called him Al.

Almost from the day he could talk, young Al Edison asked questions.

"Why is the sky blue?"

"How do birds fly?"

Mr. and Mrs. Edison tried to answer his questions, but Al kept coming up with more.

"What is lightning?"

"Why is fire hot?"

Nobody could answer all of his questions, so Al decided to find the answers by himself. When he was six years old, he tried to learn about fire by doing an experiment in the barn. The next thing he knew, the barn was burning! Al was punished by his father, but he kept right on asking questions.

When Al started school he couldn't keep his mind on his studies, so Mrs. Edison decided to teach him at home. Before long he was reading science books all by himself. He read a book of experiments that could be done at home. His bedroom became his laboratory. Young Al Edison would try anything—even mixing strange chemicals just to see what would happen. Soon the Edison home was filled with terrible odors!

His mother put a stop to that. She told Al to move his smelly, dangerous chemicals to a corner of the cellar. There the bad smells would not fill the whole house.

One day Al mixed some chemicals that he thought would make people fly. He convinced a friend to drink the mixture. The friend got very sick. Once again, Al Edison was punished.

He learned to be more careful, but he kept on experimenting.

Al was fascinated by the telegraph. In the days before telephones, the telegraph was the only way to send messages quickly from one part of the country to another. A telegrapher could move a signal through miles of wire by sending a series of long or short electrical bursts. At the other end of the wire, another telegrapher would read the electrical bursts as dots and dashes. The dots and dashes translated into words. This system is called *Morse code*. When he was eleven years old, Al built his own telegraph machine and taught himself Morse code.

MORSE CODE

A .—
B —...
C —.—.
D —..
E .
F ..—.
G ——.
H ....
I ..
J .———
K —.—
L .—..
M ——
N —.
O ———
P .——.
Q ——.—
R .—.

S ...
T —
U ..—
V ...—
W .——
X —..—
Y —.——
Z ——..
1 .————
2 ..———
3 ...——
4 ....—
5 .....
6 —....
7 ——...
8 ———..
9 ————.
0 —————

Al needed money to pay for his chemicals and machine parts. He got a job selling candy and newspapers to train passengers. Al soon earned enough money to buy his supplies. But he spent so much time working on the train he didn't have time for his experiments.

That didn't stop Al Edison.

He moved his experiments to a corner of the baggage car, creating the world's first traveling laboratory!

"Everything comes to him who hustles while he waits."
Thomas A. Edison

A Serious Setback

One morning Al overslept. The train started to leave the station without him! He ran after it holding an armload of newspapers. The conductor reached down, grabbed him by the ears, and pulled him on board.

Al heard something go SNAP! inside his head.

The next day Al couldn't hear very well. He couldn't hear the singing of a bird, or the train's whistle. He could hear voices, but when people whispered or mumbled, he couldn't understand them.

Did Al Edison give up because he couldn't hear? Not at all. He worked harder than ever. He said the silence made it easier for him to think.

People who *persevere* learn to keep on trying when bad things happen. Ludwig van Beethoven, one of the greatest composers of all time, also lost his hearing. He went on to create some of the greatest music ever.

The Tramp Telegrapher

When he was 15, Edison went to work as a telegrapher. He had trouble hearing voices, but he could hear the clicking of the telegraph machine. He became a "tramp telegrapher," traveling from town to town and working one job after another.

"Restlessness and discontent are the necessities of progress."
Thomas A. Edison

At first, Edison was slow and clumsy. He didn't know how to spell many words. He was not very good at his work, but he kept trying to do better.

He invented a new kind of handwriting that helped him write down telegraph messages faster. He practiced his spelling and he learned to send messages quickly. After a lot of hard work, Edison became one of the best telegraphers in the country. He was offered an important job with Western Union in Boston.

Edison worked as a telegrapher by day, but he spent his nights working on his inventions. He finally decided to quit his job with Western Union so he could work full time as an inventor.

Edison the Inventor

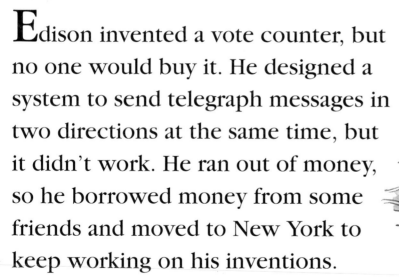

Edison invented a vote counter, but no one would buy it. He designed a system to send telegraph messages in two directions at the same time, but it didn't work. He ran out of money, so he borrowed money from some friends and moved to New York to keep working on his inventions.

He spent what little money he had for supplies. Because he was nearly broke, he lived on apple dumplings and coffee, a meal he could buy for a nickel. Times were hard, but Edison kept right on working on his inventions.

He invented a machine called a "gold ticker" for keeping track of gold prices. Western Union liked his idea and paid him $15,000 for his invention. Finally, one of his inventions had paid off.

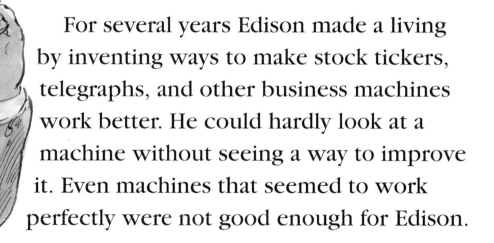

For several years Edison made a living by inventing ways to make stock tickers, telegraphs, and other business machines work better. He could hardly look at a machine without seeing a way to improve it. Even machines that seemed to work perfectly were not good enough for Edison.

"Show me a thoroughly satisfied man and I will show you a failure."
Thomas A. Edison

During the 1870s, Edison became known as a successful inventor. He invented the *Mimeograph*, a type of copying machine. He invented a box that would automatically send a signal for help in case of home emergencies. He invented a motorized electric pen that could copy documents quickly.

Edison had lots of good ideas, but he never seemed to have enough money. He finally figured out a way to send telegraphs in two directions at the same time over a single wire. But the telegraph company that bought it did not pay him all it owed. His money problems grew worse. Most people would have given up and gone back to working a regular job, but not Thomas Alva Edison! He borrowed more money, moved to Menlo Park, New Jersey, and built a huge barn. There, with a few poorly paid helpers, Edison went to work on his greatest inventions. At Menlo Park, Edison's three greatest ideas came to life.

Two-Way Telegraph

The Phonograph

In 1876, there was no way to preserve a sound. There were no tape recorders or CD players. When someone played a piece of music, it was gone forever. No one would ever hear it again. When a great speech was delivered, only the people who were there would ever hear the speaker's voice.

Edison had an idea. He wondered if a human voice could be stored on a piece of waxed paper. If the sound vibrations of a voice were transferred to a sensitive needle and inscribed into the waxed paper, would the sound be preserved? Edison thought that by reversing the process, the pattern on the waxed paper could be transferred back through the needle to an amplifier and heard once again.

His early experiments failed. The first recording efforts sounded like dogs growling and cats screeching. For months, Edison and his helpers tried to capture the human voice. After many failures, they replaced the waxed paper with tin foil wrapped around a cylinder. On December 6, 1987, Edison spoke into the machine:

Mary had a little lamb
Her-fleece was white as snow

As his helpers gathered around the machine, Edison turned the foil cylinder. Though he had lost most of his hearing, he recognized the sound of his own voice.

"Mary had a little lamb" the machine said.

Even Edison could hardly believe it. For the first time in history, a sound had been captured, then played back. The phonograph was born!

"Genius is one per cent inspiration
and ninety-nine per cent perspiration."
Thomas A. Edison

His Brightest Idea

Have you ever tried to read by candlelight? The light shivers and dances and is not very bright. Your eyes get tired, your head aches, and candle wax drips all over your book!

In the 1800s, if you wanted to read a book after dark, you had to read by the light of a flame.

Thomas Edison wanted to change that.

Scientists knew that running an electric current through a thin wire, or filament, would make the filament glow brightly. The problem was that the filament would get so hot, it would quickly melt or burn up. The light would last only a few seconds. Inventors had been trying to develop a filament that would glow but not burn up. They all failed.

Failure did not bother Thomas Edison. Each time he failed it brought him closer to success.

"Results! Why man, I have gotten a lot of results. I know several thousand things that won't work."

Thomas A. Edison

Edison made a filament of carbon-coated paper, but it burned up. He tried platinum wire, but the wire melted. He sealed the filament inside a glass bulb and sucked out all the air. The filament lasted longer, but within a few minutes it would burn out. Edison and the researchers at Menlo Park tested over one thousand different filaments. For two years, they struggled with the problem.

Finally, in October of 1879, Edison tried a cotton thread coated with carbon powder.

He sealed it inside a glass bulb.

He turned on the electric current.

The light burned for 40 hours!

"If it can burn that many hours, I know I can make it burn a hundred," Edison declared.

And so he did. Today's light bulbs can burn for many hundreds of hours.

Let's Go to the Movies!

The phonograph let people store sounds and listen to them again whenever they wanted. Edison wondered whether he could do the same thing with pictures.

Photography had been invented many years before, but no one knew a way to make the pictures move. Edison thought he could capture motion by taking a series of photographs very quickly, then playing them back at the same speed. The problem was to create a camera that would take hundreds of pictures every minute.

As usual, his early efforts failed. He had trouble with the camera, the film, and the lighting. After many months of labor, the Menlo Park team finally built a camera and a machine they called a *Kinetoscope.* Then they built the world's first movie studio. It was a small building on pivots that could be moved to capture the light as the sun moved across the sky. Edison and his crew started making short movies.

One of the first movies they made was *The Edison Kinetoscopic Record of a Sneeze.* It was a very short movie that showed a man sneezing. Today, this does not sound like a very interesting movie, but back then people were amazed. They had never seen moving pictures before.

"Kinetoscopic records" were not shown on a big screen like today's movies. You had to go to a *Kinetoscope parlor*, put a nickel into a machine, then look through a peephole to view a movie that would last only half a minute or so.

People came by the thousands to see this amazing new invention. Once again, one of Edison's ideas would change the world.

A New World

Thomas Alva Edison lived for 40 years after inventing the motion picture camera. He kept on inventing until he was too old and sick to leave his home. He and his Menlo Park team went on to invent hundreds of new products, many of which we still use today.

Young Al Edison grew up in a world without electric lights, telephones, automobiles, CD players, movies, or radios. People read books by candlelight. They kept their food cold with blocks of ice. They traveled in horse-drawn wagons. And no one knew that one day people would be able to fly.

When he died on October 18, 1931, all of that had changed. It was a bright new world, and Thomas Edison had helped build it.

Edison was a great inventor. But what made him so successful? He was smart, creative, and inventive . . . but so are a lot of other people. Perhaps his greatest gift was his ability to persevere. Where others would have given up, Edison just kept on trying. It took him 1,000 tries to create the electric light bulb. What if he had quit after 999? Would you be reading this book by candlelight?

Study Guide

Reading about famous or successful people can help us live our own lives. Sometimes we learn from their mistakes, and sometimes we learn from their successes. Thomas Edison's life was filled with both.

1. Which of these qualities do you think are most important?

Intelligence	Strength
Athletic ability	Alertness
Imagination	Honesty
Generosity	Perseverance
Humor	Curiosity
Health	Kindness
Patience	Fairness
Courage	Self-confidence

Which qualities do you think were most important to Thomas Edison?

2. Do you think Thomas Edison ever got angry and frustrated? When one of his light bulbs didn't work, what do you think he did?

   a. Screamed and threw it on the floor and stomped it to bits

   b. Went fishing

   c. Built another light bulb

3. Thomas Edison did many foolish and dangerous things when he was a boy, but he always learned from his experiences. Later in life, when an experiment failed, he felt that his failure brought him closer to a solution. Can you think of an example of how making a mistake helps you learn to do something right?

4. Edison succeeded as an inventor even though he was nearly deaf. Many other men and women have overcome disabilities and gone on to do great things. Can you name any other disabled people who became famous?

5. During Edison's time, many other people were creating important new inventions. Can you name two?

Study Guide Answers

1. There is no right answer to this question. All of these things are important, and none of them is any good without the others. For instance, what good would it be to have tremendous strength is you did not have the intelligence to know what to do with it? And what good is imagination without the self-confidence to put it to work? Thomas Edison had tremendous creativity, but without his perseverance, patience, and courage, his ideas would have just floated around in his head!

2. Everybody gets mad and frustrated at times. Even Thomas Edison. Although we do not know for sure, it is possible that a few of his bad light bulbs got thrown on the floor and stomped on! But what happened next is more important, because if Edison *did* have a temper tantrum, he probably swept up the broken bulb and started building a new one right away.

3. Have you ever practiced shooting a basketball or jumping rope? Have you ever missed? Each time you try to shoot that ball through the hoop and miss, you are becoming a better shot. Every time that jump rope catches on your foot, you are learning to jump faster or higher. Until we learn to do things wrong, it is hard to know how to do them right.

4. People with disabilities are often able to overcome their physical limitations and go on to reach their goals. Many of them have become famous for their work. Here are just a few examples:

Helen Keller lost her sight and her hearing when she was only 19 months old. She learned to read Braille and to write using a special typewriter. In 1904, Helen Keller graduated from Radcliffe College and spent the rest of her life writing and speaking to help other disabled people.

Franklin Delano Roosevelt, a rising young politician, was stricken with polio in 1921. For most of his life, he had to wear leg braces or sit in a wheelchair, yet he went on to serve four terms as the president of the United States.

Stephen W. Hawking, the famous British physicist, has been in a wheelchair for many years. Since 1985, Hawking has been unable to talk. He uses a computerized speech synthesizer to communicate. He wrote a book called *A Brief History of Time*.

5. There were many thousands of inventions by other people during Edison's lifetime. Some of the most famous were the **airplane** (invented by the Wright brothers), the **telephone** (invented by Alexander Graham Bell), the **radio** (invented by Guglielmo Marconi), and the **automobile** (different types of autos were invented by many different people, but Henry Ford made the first inexpensive, mass-produced automobile). Although no other inventor of Edison's time invented as many different things as Edison, they all shared one thing: They had an idea, and they never gave up.

Thomas Alva Edison Time Line

February 11, 1847   Thomas Alva Edison is born in Milan, Ohio

1857   Al becomes interested in books on chemistry. He is allowed to set up a laboratory in his family's basement.

1859   Al moves his laboratory to an empty train car on the Grand Trunk Railway. He also begins to print a newspaper he calls the Grand Trunk Herald.

1868   Al moves to Boston, Massachusetts to work for Western Union.

1876   Edison builds a new laboratory in Menlo Park, New Jersey.

1877   Edison invents the carbon-button transmitter and the cylinder phonograph.

1879   Thomas Edison invents the light bulb.

1887   Al moves to West Orange, New Jersey. He builds a new laboratory and continues working on the phonograph.

1913   Edison invents the first talking motion picture.

October 18, 1931   Thomas Alva Edison dies at his West Orange, New Jersey home.